# What is soft?

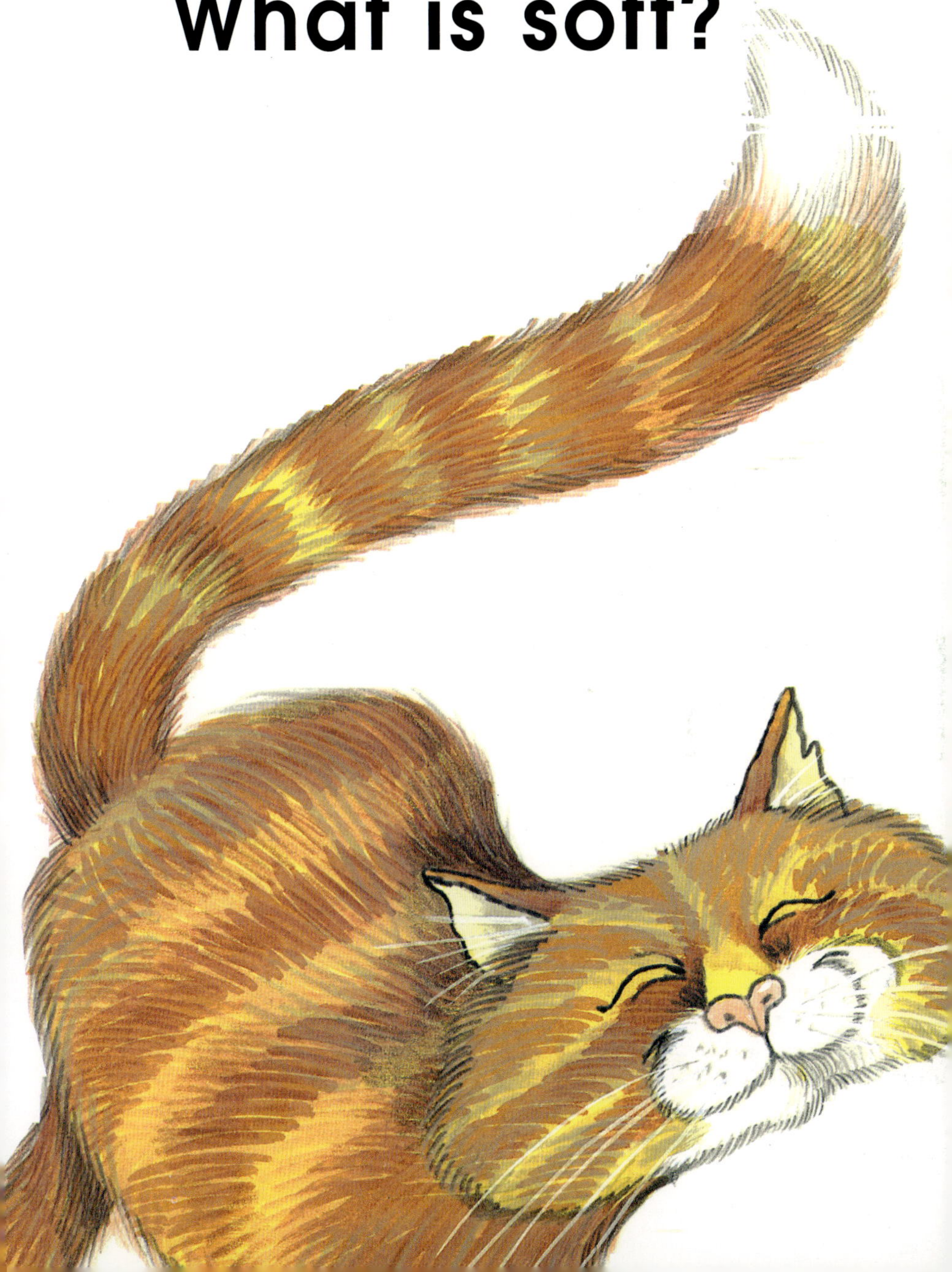

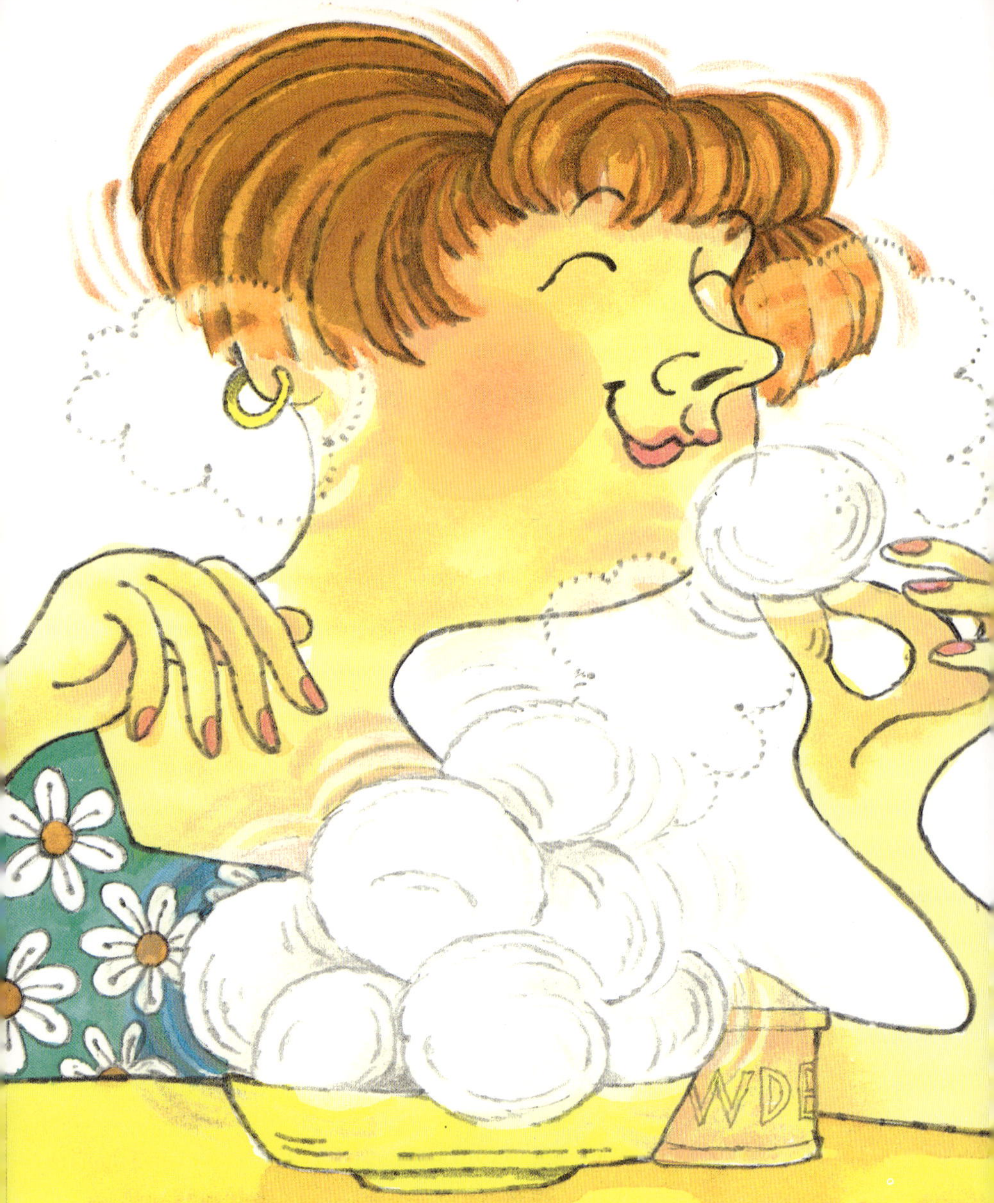

Cotton is soft.

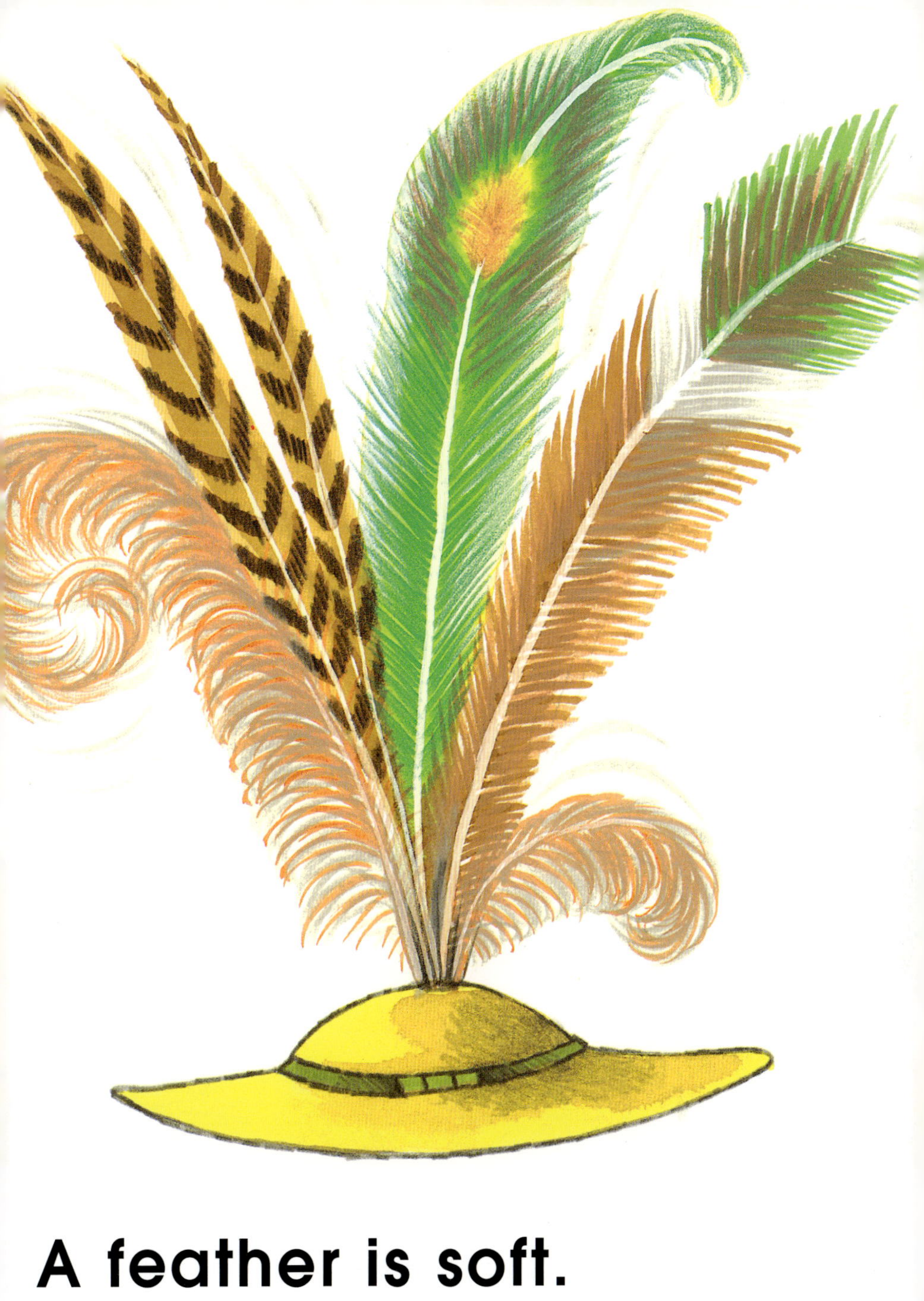

A feather is soft.

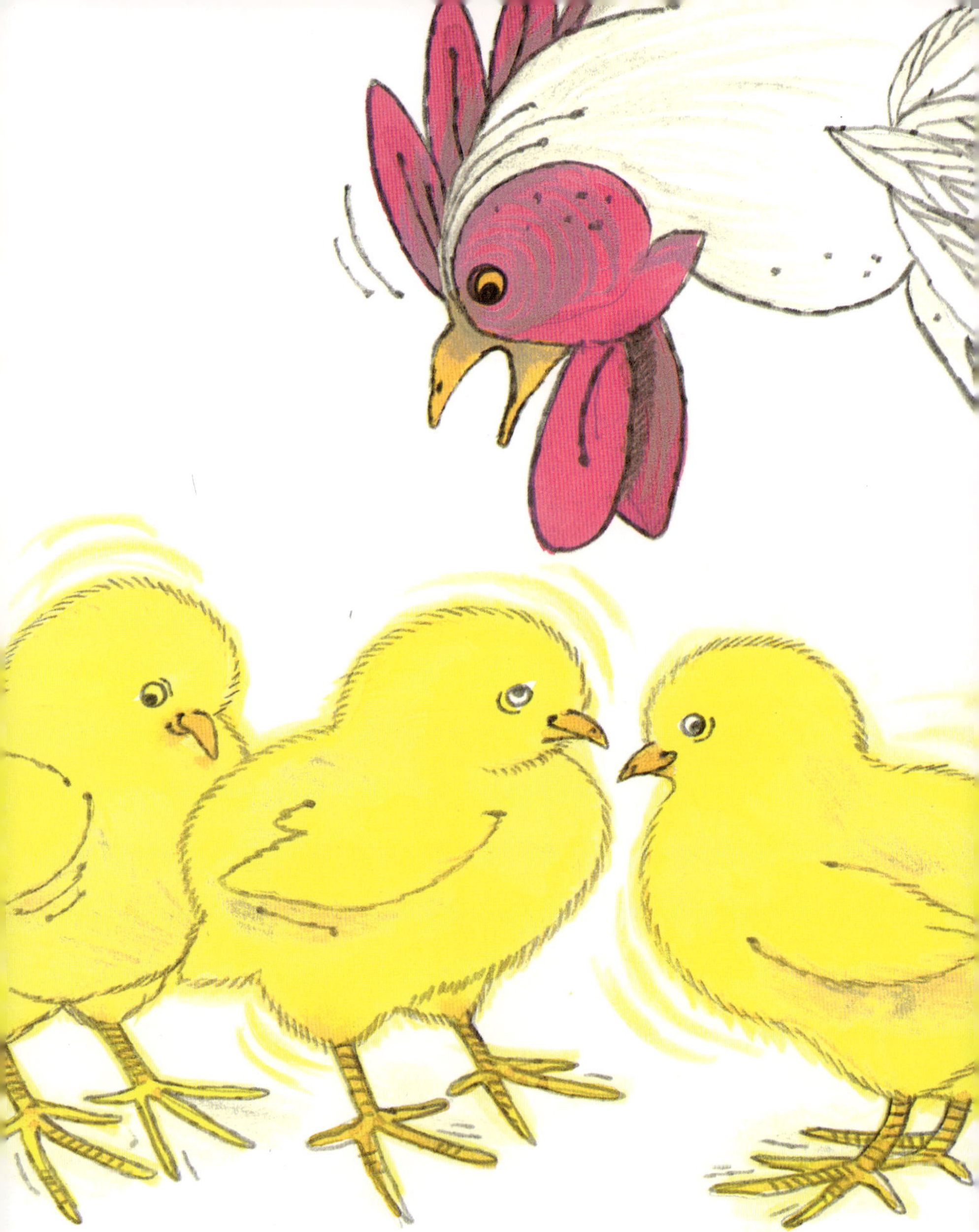

A chicken is soft.

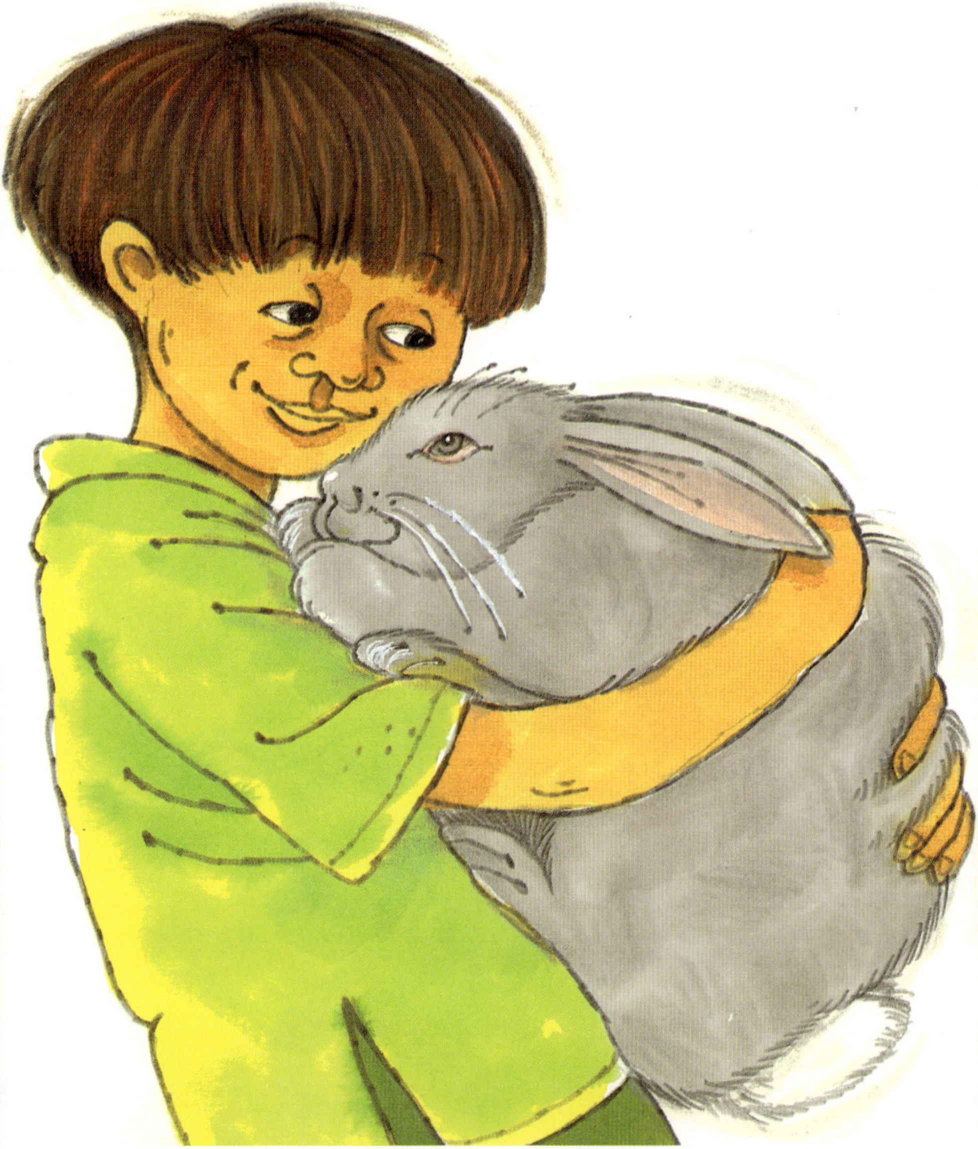

A rabbit is soft.

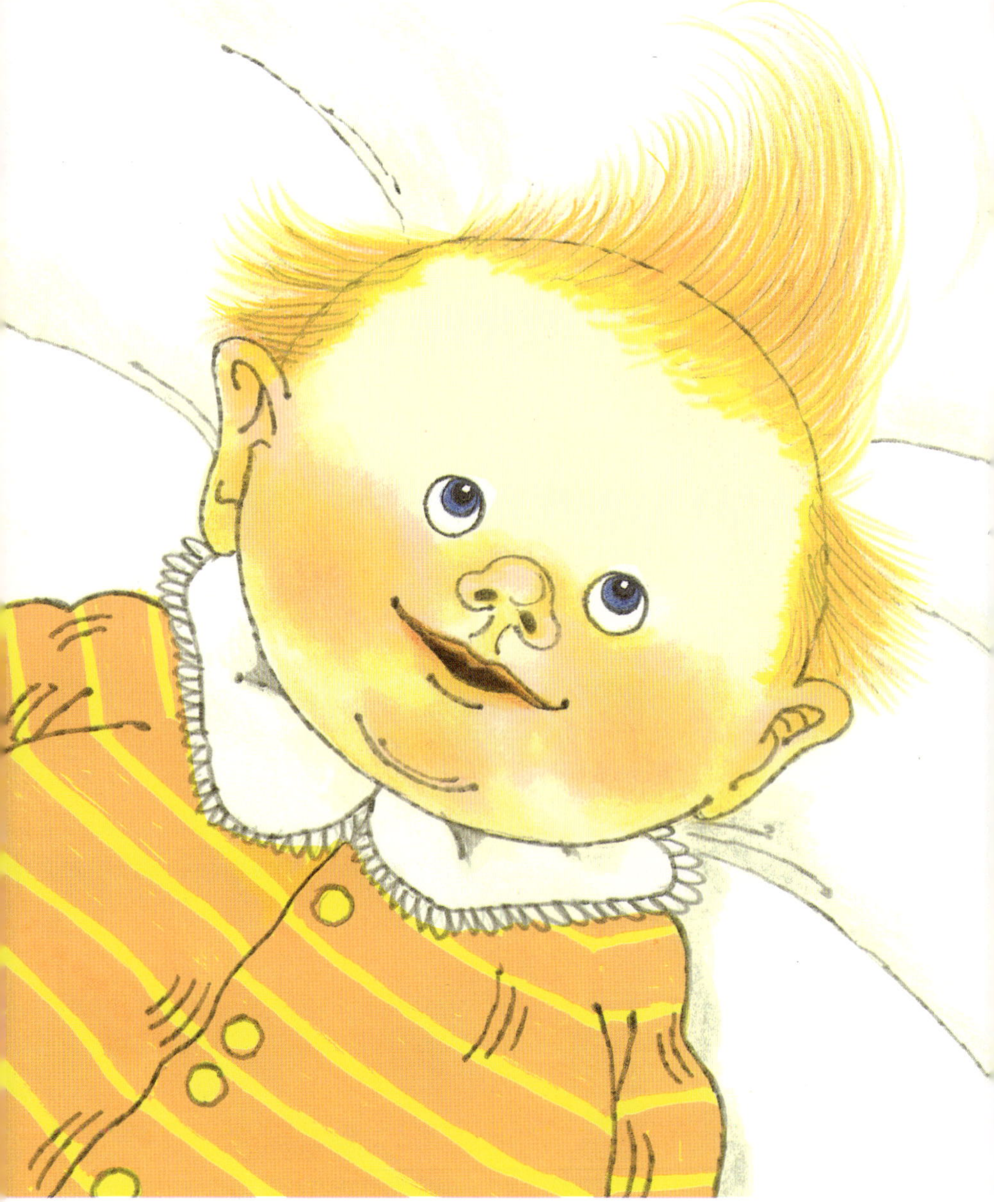

A baby's hair is soft.

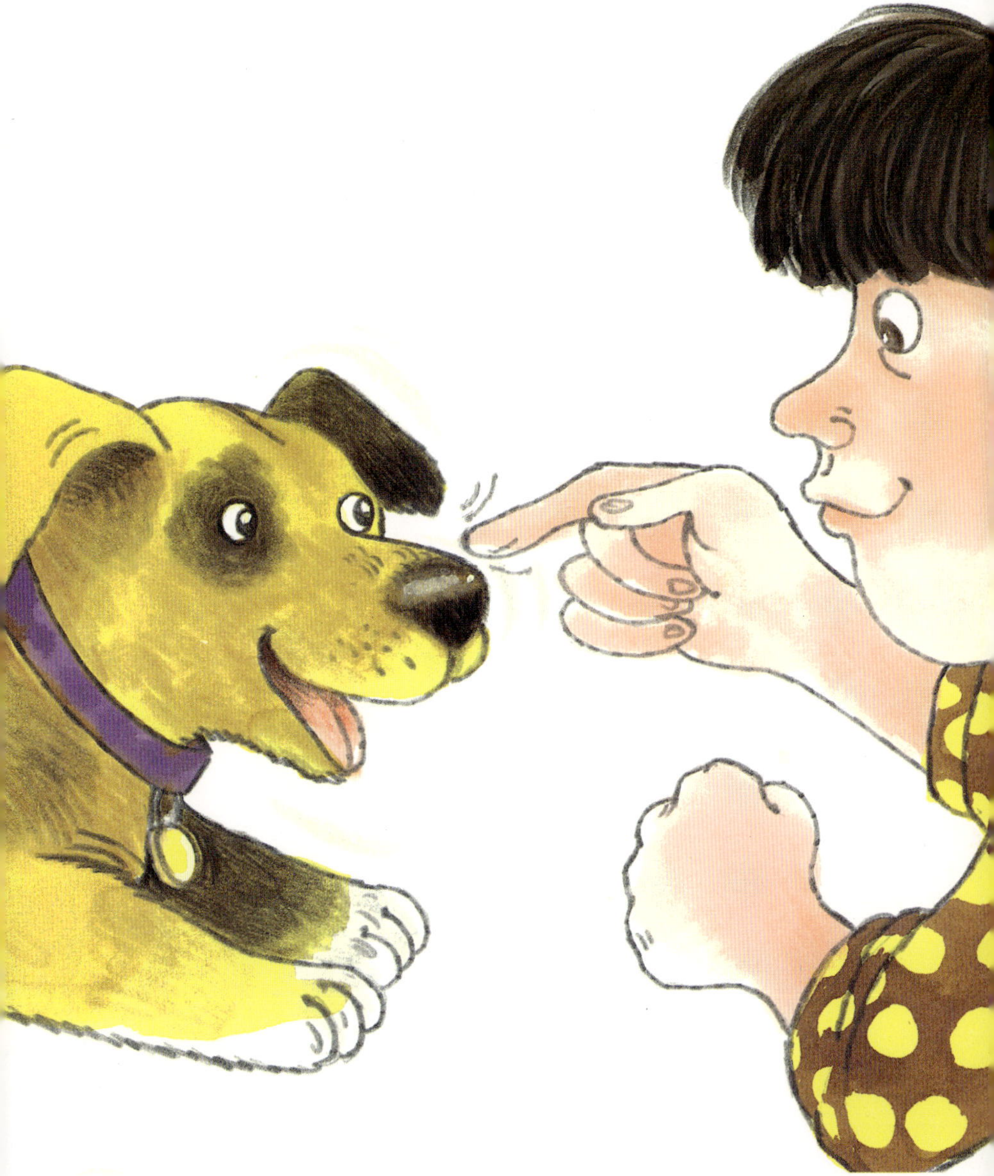

A puppy's nose is soft.

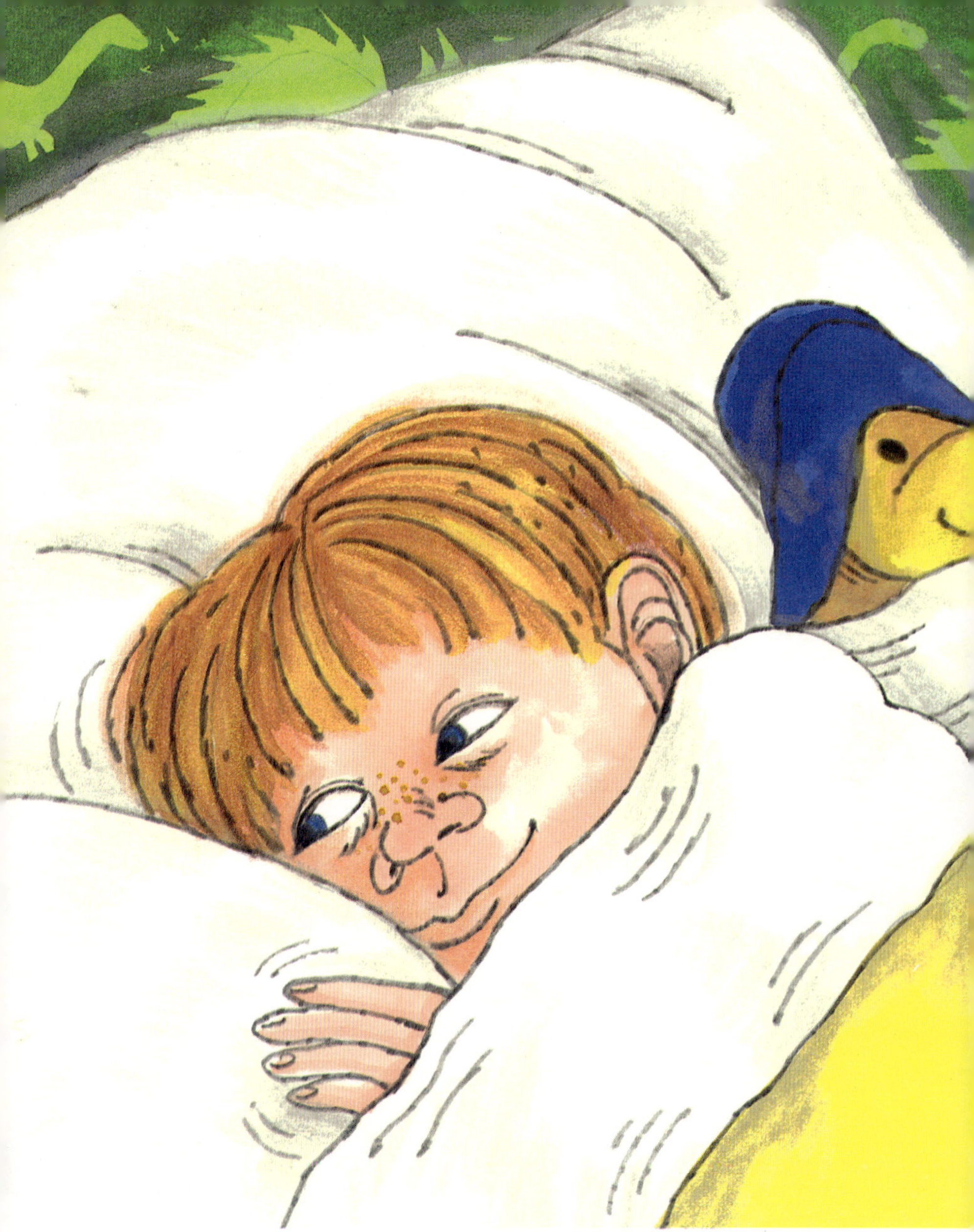

My pillow is soft.
Goodnight!